AN INTERPRETATION
OF
BRAZILIAN LITERATURE

VIANNA MOOG

*Translated
by*
JOHN KNOX

GREENWOOD PRESS, PUBLISHERS
WESTPORT, CONNECTICUT

Originally published in 1951
by Service of Publications, Rio de Janeiro

First Greenwood Reprinting 1970

Library of Congress Catalogue Card Number 70-98881

SBN 8371-3156-1

Printed in the United States of America

AN INTERPRETATION

OF

BRAZILIAN LITERATURE

I

What does Brazilian literature consist in? What are its characteristics and tendencies? Does it constitute a homogeneous whole, capable of being defined, or is it still in the vague, confused phase of indeterminations? Is it possessed of stable, permanent values enabling it to survive the transformations through which the world is passing?

Face to face with these queries and the themes which they suggest, I sometimes ask myself with anxiety whether I am not proceeding along the lines of the Greeks of the Late Empire, who delighted in debating the essence of light and the sex of the angels, while the barbarians were hammering at the gates of the city. Obviously, this doubt is inconsistent, and indeed the analogy is merely apparent. Nowadays, when we are all living with our eyes fixed on the future, in a search for signs and portents, in the vague, restless hope of surprising therein the tendency of the world that is hastening towards us, these and other questions must crowd in on all those who, with a touch of sensibility to be moved, a minimum of nerves to vibrate and a residuum of hope to believe, still have faith, in the midst of the universal landslide of so many sacred things, in the possibility of saving from the great disaster, the moral and spiritual values which are dear to them. And in so doing, they are in no way indulging in Byzantine speculation. Rather, at a moment when all that is heard is the clamor of the oppressed, the menace of death and the heart-rending cries of despair, are they pledging a vow of confidence in the unraveling of the skein of time and of belief in the perpetuation of the values of the spirit.

This brings me back to my questions: What does Brazilian literature consist in? What are its fundamental characteristics? What are its tendencies? Is it possessed of stable, permanent values, enabling it to survive the transformations through which the world is passing? Does it constitute a homogeneous whole, capable of being defined, or is it still in the vague, confused phase of indeterminations?

Strangely enough, the same queries as regards French, German, Spanish or Portuguese literature do not seem to me to offer such great obstacles. In the case of French literature, for instance, I am convinced that no brilliant stroke of intuition is required to proclaim from the outset that we are dealing with a literature, the chief trait of which is the Cartesian sense of measure and clarity; that in this literature of rationalists and essayists, it is the Cartesian way of thinking, inseparable from the French *esprit,* that has forged, unbroken and unvarying, the perfect chain of continuity and intimate spiritual relationship from Descartes to Pascal, Pascal to Montaigne, Montaigne to Voltaire, Voltaire to Anatole France. As to German literature, there is no great difficulty in maintaining its philosophical and metaphysical nature, the feature that links Luther to Kant, Kant to Goethe, Goethe to Nietsche and Nietsche to Spengler. In Spanish literature I need only stress its mystic and chivalrous character, to draw near to the substantial verity that lies therein as much as do the lyrical heroics in Portuguese and the sublimation of temporal and spatial realities in the case of the English writers. This is not much, I know, but it is already something. From these points of vantage, it is relatively easy to obtain a comprehensive view of each of them.

But, whereas it is possible to establish points of reference for the conception of those matured literatures that make up the mutual heritage of western culture, the same cannot be said of Brazilian literature. In this domain, the problems become more and more confused, and our queries drift hither and thither, void of solution. In point of fact, wherein lies the predominant trait? Have we a literature of essayists, like France? Or imaginatives, like the English? Lyrical, heroical, like Portuguese literature, whence it sprang? For my part, I shall not dare to give a categorically definite reply to any of these questions, for the very reason that, if we really come down to it, there is no possibility of gleaning from the mass of Brazilian literature, any wide-scale truth, any noble synthesis to be contined within the rigor of a definition.

As we are not in the presence of a homogeneous, neatly defined whole, cut and dried like a European literature, in order to comprehend and to interpret Brazil's literary work, we must abandon the intention, from the outset, of embracing it in its entirety from a general standpoint. Above all, should we treat with due reserve the chronological process, according to which it has been studied up till now. I even think that it is high time to set it on one side. The further I advance in our histories of literature the more I am convinced that the chronological process; which may indeed be said to be the only one which has been applied thereto, is not that which is the best adapted to an accurate comprehension of the secrets of our literature. As a criterium, it may be very valuable in the case of literatures which are more or less homogeneous, such as the French, Spanish, Italian or English literatures. However, it is not fitted to the study of one that, despite a unity of language and origin, is condemned by geographical differentiations, by those of the form of production, of climate and of culture, to a bewildering diversity. The chronological process is also of some value to whoever may be content to demand of the history of a literature nothing more than a more or less extensive table of consecrated values, a bibliographical schedule, a mere catalog of authors and their works; it is not so, however, for those who search, therein, not only information, but essential verities bearing on our history, our spiritual formation and above all, our destiny. From this point of view, the chronological method has already exhausted its possibilities. It has nothing more to give. It may yet serve, if at all, to decorate partial truths proclaiming our lack of originality with regard to European movements, a consequence of the other half-truth which endeavors to present the American as a man that is European in all that is deep and stratified in him, and merely American in his superficial layers. Since, then, the chronological process has shown itself incapable of offering new contributions to the study of Brazilian literature, above all for those who take pleasure in thinking generously about themes that should not elsewise be pondered, it is now time to look for some other system, in the assurance that every subject, however complex, always has a method which is eminently suited to its complexities.

What, then, is the interpretive system, which is the most convenient? In my opinion, we must resort to the analysis of the cultural nuclei, the sum of which forms the heterogeneous framework of the so-called Brazilian literature. Split up Brazil into regions dominated by the same climate, the same geographical conditions, the same forms of production, and the problem is immediately simplified. Wherever these factors are conjugated to a certain degree of homogeneity, it may be safely concluded that a definite homogeneous cultural nucleus will be found, forming as it were a separate unit of Brazilian literature taken as a whole. For, from this viewpoint, despite our territorial continuity, Brazil does not form a continent; we are a cultural archipelago. And this archipelago is made up of many cultural islands, all more or less autonomous and distinct.

II

The first of the Islands of the archipelago, in geographical order, is Amazonia. Formed by two of the largest States of Brazil, Amazonas and Pará, part of Mato Grosso, and by scraps of territory borrowed from six other districts, it is entirely surrounded by the bulwarks of various mountain ranges. To the north, the rising heights of the Guianas; to the south, the Brazilian plateau; and to the west, the barrier of the Andes. But it is not without an effort that the most daring imaginations, from fragment to fragment, succeed in building up this gigantic setting. It would seem easier to accept unquestioningly that the light of the stars takes immeasurable years to glide through the infinity of space, than to conceive that on so small a planet as the earth, there may be room for the cosmic immensity of the Amazon valley. Without a broken horizon, with neither hill nor jagged crest to provide the imagination with some landmark short of the encircling horseshoe band of granite; sealed, impenetrable, people with mystery; the realm of unyielding Nature; mute, jealous of thought and body — confronting this scene, man ever trembles with cosmic terror. Face to face with a strange, crowded landscape that has none of the charm of beauty that calms and rests the senses, to offset that horrifying splendor which crushes and intimidates the soul of man, how could the sentiment that dominates him be otherwises? The marshland labyrinth, knit by the unending forest in warp and woof, the solemn silence from space to space, the germinal anguish of the earth in her never-ceasing struggle with the waters, now streaked with mud, now black, the persistent murmur of the wavelets and the twisted contortions of the forest lands, the brutality of caving banks, the sudden storms, grim and terrifying — all is an ever-present witness to the rage with which the fatal powers of destruction burst upon the valley. In other worlds, man may hold gentle commerce with nature, enter the precincts of the land with sentiments of confidence and pantheistic devotion. Here, no. In Amazonia, where danger is everywhere, on land, in the water and in the air, man will never be a pagan in the hellenic sense of the word. Molested and belittled by his surroundings, Amazonia inspires him first and foremost with the longing to unveil her secrets. Everything else fades into the background of the reality which hems him in. To elucidate these secrets, men of wisdom are thrust onwards to the most daring of conjectures, whilst those unarmed with laws and formulas, cling desperately to myth and legend. Hence the literature of the Amazon: a literature exclusively dealing with an interpretation of the land itself. Whether the writers are born there, whether they are writers from other States or foreigners, not one escapes the domination of cosmic terror.

To illustrate this assertion, we have the case of Euclides da Cunha. He goes to the Amazon as leader of a boundary commission. His task is to mark frontiers. Suddenly, on the very verge of the plain, he is amazed, at the mouth of the Amazon, with the anti-national character of the great river, rolling to far-off lands, in the form of alluvial soil, the lands of Brazil. Once past the mouth, the cosmic terror has him in its grip, overwhelming him with a desperate saraband of interrogations. Can Amazonia be the first or the last chapter of Genesis, the first or the last day of creation? To these and other questions, he replies in his nervous style, with those tragic accents, that drag back his prose to the epoch of the Old Testament prophets.

But not only Euclides, nerves twinging and stricken, a permanent victim to a diseased and exaggerative imagination, succumbs to the sortilege. All the writers that have struggled through those glades, whether national or foreign, poets or plain chroniclers, geologists, ethnologists or botanists, from Wallace to Humboldt, from Alexandre Rodrigues Ferreira to Gonçalves Dias, from Inglês de Sousa to Tavares Bastos, from Alberto Rangel to Gastão Cruls, all, without exception, pay tribute to the cosmic emotion. Not to fall under its sway, it is of no avail to have been born in the heart of Amazonia, to have lived in the apparent intimacy of the great plain. It is enough to see what happened to Raimundo de Morais, without doubt and despite the tangled obscurity of his style, one of the most expressive figures in the literature of the Amazon. Never did Amazonia allow his imagination a moment's respite and his whole life was of little scope to exhaust the problems that she thrust before him. Nor did she abandon her hold on the imagination of Gastão Cruls, who has never succeeded in breaking free. Whoever has ventured near the plain, remains forever enthralled. Amazonia, like Antinea in the legend of lost Atlantis, after gripping the imagination of a mere mortal, binds him forever a prisoner to her tragic seduction and to her spell. None can resist nor rebel. Only surrender. . . . Or else, resort to flight; and this is, indeed, the dominating thought.

III

The Northeast is different. It is true that the element of Nature is important, but it is not permanent, nor omnipresent, as in Amazonia, and it only becomes predominant in times of drought. When winter fails to arrive, and the sunbaked earth burns black what used to be splendidly green, then indeed the natural element gains sway. In order to avert or to soften it, all the saints of the brushwood calendar are called into action. Throughout the backwoods, processions surge forward in a picturesque confusion of Christianity and Paganism. No one, however, abandons the land — as in Amazonia, where the idea of flight is almost an obsession — before the resources of liturgy and religious ritual are fully exhausted. Only in the last extreme, does the grim march of retreat begin. A legion of hunger-stricken beings, men that were, throng the trails in one last effort to reach the coast. Weakened by suffering, they linger out along the roadsides, where roughhewn, nameless crosses are the only memorials of these strange perigrinations of living ghosts. With the fall of the rains, though, to hasten back is the one thought in their minds. Relinquishment was slow, but the return is precipitate and the backwoods light up anew with the ready smile of prosperity. As by enchantment, the earthborn anguish vanishes, and with it the drought literature of its most vivid narrators, José Américo de Almeida, Graciliano Ramos and Raquel de Queirós.

But, positively, the predominant factor of the Northeastern cultural group is not cosmic. A visit to the principal towns of the northeast coast suffices to prove that the literature sprung therefrom is of a very different nature. The striking contrasts between the man of means and the valued slave, urban survival of the rural contrast between veranda'd house — the "great house" — and Negro huts, between rich and poor, white and black, situated at the two extremes of a wondrous diversity of races, all point towards the conclusion that here the social aspect could never be ignored. Social and class literature. Polemics and pamphlets, revolution and romanticism. A literature or landowners and proletarians. Lords of the land, with Joaquim Nabuco and Oliveira Lima. Sympathisers with the outcast and the oppressed, like José Lins do Rêgo and Graciliano Ramos. Gilberto Freire, linking the aristocrat with the masses, the town with the backwoods. Indeed, Gilberto Freire, insofar as he represents a type of culture, is Northeastern. As much in his patriarchal moods as in his populism, he belongs to the Northeast, even in his perhaps unconscious yearning after the Brazil of Imperial days which marked the apogee of the civilization that had grown up with the Masters of the plantations, from whose stock he himself has sprung. Herein lies no definite incompatibility with the Republic, as may be noted in the works of Joaquim Nabuco and Oliveira Lima, who only feel spiritually at ease in the cultural domain of the Regal Colony and the Empire, which nurtured those two monuments of Brazilian literature: *Um estadista do Império* and *D. João VI no Brasil* (A Statesman of the Empire and Dom John the Sixth in Brazil). But it is easy to see that the artificial industrialism of the Republic, encouraged in the South to the detriment of the North, by the imposition of protective tariffs, provocative of reprisals on the part of the industrial countries, thereby humbling patriarchal Brazil to ruin and decadence, inspires him with neither sympathy, nor enthusiasm. The world that he loves is that of the "great house", the monasteries, church festivals and country fairs, the old family mansions, blue tile buildings and wrought iron balconies. The paleontologist reconstructs a prehistoric monster from a fragment of bone; the geologist conjures up a period in the formation of the earth's crust from a mere handful of clay; a leaflet, a blossom or a tiny pistil, suggests to the botanist all the diverse vegetation of a certain zone; so Gilberto Freire, with a scrap of parchment, an aging manor or a ruined fountain, intertwined with a touch of ivy, revives in his enchanting frescoes all the beauty of a world long past. For all his true affection is centered in the Great House. The author of *Sobrados e Mucambos* (Plantation Mansions and Family Slaves) — like José Lins do Rêgo, who is creating in fiction what Freire has created in the field of sociology, and like Joaquim Nabuco — carries his "Massangana" deep-rooted in his soul. And since "Massangana" could not exist elsewhere, but only in the Northeast, Gilberto Freire cannot conceive of a life apart. In his attachment to the land, he reminds one in some ways of a prominent personality of Tierra del Fuego, cited by Gustave Le Bon. This personality, sent to England one day to be instructed in the ways of

European culture and to be turned out a perfect gentleman, returned after some time to the country of his birth, where, a year later, this flower of the upper classes was to be found naked and happy in his former mode of living, declaring that he had no desire ever to return to the homes of civilization. Like the savage of Terra del Fuego, Gilberto Freire would not barter away his Northeast for the splendors of any civilization. The Northeast is the spatial medium for his meditations. For his social researches, it is the ideal laboratory.

IV

Whereas the literature of the Northeast is marked by its sociological trends, that of Bahia may be distinguished from it, as an initial contrast, by precisely the absence of this feature. It is above all a literature of the erudite, humanists and dilettantes, rather than a literature inclined towards social and organic ends. Spiritually a daughter of the XVIIIth century, the century *par excellence* of humanism and eruditeness endowed with a gentle climate and unworried by the sting of bitter problems, Bahia could give herself up freely to the style of life typified by that epoch. Why endeavor to lay bare the meaning of the land, when there were still so many Greek and Latin epigrams to verify? Why allow oneself to be impressed by real problems, when there was so little time to read the classics, and sacred and profane history? It was by no means despicable not to possess any opinions on the future of the race, on the consequences of slavery, on the social conflicts to be engendered thereby. What really was crude and unpardonable was to be unaware of the latest European novelty, not to delight in the palest passages of Virgil or Homer, not to appreciate the subtle renderings of grammarians and masters of theology, to ignore the slightest rule of rhetoric. To be unacquainted with a Portuguese classic meant at that time a sentence of social ostracism, so great was the shame and iniquity of it. Of course the backwoods did exist, together with bandits, fanatics and their crimes. But the backwoods were far too far off to need anyone to bother about them. Besides, the backwoods were locked away in the Northeast and, therefore, lay quite beyond the scope of the cogitations of Bahia. So long as prosperity and wealth abounded, so long as vessels continued to cast anchor, laden with slaves from the coast of Africa, there was nothing to do but plunge one's intelligence in the marvels of the time being and prepare one's sons to shine in court circles. Brilliancy at court! And the Jesuit colleges were there, right at hand, to mold the pride of the family, those infant prodigies, those sparkling minds, that later would discard the habits of adolescence and become grave, learned, respected speakers, omniscient. None were better fitted than the Jesuits to bring up these portentous youngsters, that were all charm and wonder to patriarchal Brazil. It is true that from time to time there happened what is now happening in the case of Hermes Lima, Pedro Calmon and Jorge Amado; Bahian writers do sometimes revive the traditions of the XVIIth century, when the colonial chroniclers, with Pedro Vaz Caminha in the forefront, knew how to convey their messages without a trellis-work of erudition at the expense of grace and simplicity. But, though a Castro Alves may emerge from this cultural nucleus, more in the nature of a spiritual son of the Northeast, and particularly of Recife, rather than of Bahia, just as Tobias Barreto belongs in reality to the erudite Bahia school, the truth is that up till now, Bahia, apart from one of two exceptions, has never succeeded in striking free from the unconscious moral saturation of her eruditeness. She is erudite to the core; the very atmosphere exhales erudition.

Eruditeness is her *genius loci* — that same *genius loci,* which from the days of Paracelsus, has ever imbued physical localities with a moral and cultural physiognomy to render them unmistakable; this is the vocation and the fatality of Bahia. Times change, forms and styles of living develop, governments rise and fall, institutions crash to destruction, empires are born and decay, but the *genius loci* of Bahia remains practically unaltered. When and how it came into being, nobody knows: whether with the Jesuit colleges; whether with the sermons of Antônio Vieira, who called God to count for having allowed Brazil, a Catholic country, to be invaded by the Dutch, a people of heretics; or perhaps with the passage of Dom John VI by the city of Salvador, ordering the town to be illuminated "for the Englishman to see". The fact remains that it is always to be found there. It shines dully in the eloquence of her orators, in the richness of her churches, in the style of her writers, in the *féerie* of her local festivals, in the learned nature of her writings in their multiple diversity, and above all in the science and in the culture of Rui Barbosa, the true iconography of Bahia culture.

V

It may be said: But Jesuit colleges were not a privilege of Bahia, nor is eruditeness an exclusively Bahia trend. It is indeed a phenomenon of far greater range. The cloying odor of erudition, with cultural strivings of a purely ornamental character, do truly seem to impregnate all the cultural centers of the country. And as a result in part of our patriarchal civilization, based on slavery and the ownership of vast estates, this tendency is still so deep-rooted that, in spite of the abolition of slavery, the fall of the Empire and the foundation of the Republic, it has been impossible to extirpate it. This may readily be understood. In 1888, only nominally and in very limited aspects, was slavery abolished. Moreover, despite the elimination of slave labor, we persisted in cultivating a varied array of prejudices against work in many forms, much as the Roman patricians did. According to the national view of the question, not every form of activity dignifies man. On the contrary, a large, indeed a formidable, number, of such forms degrade him. Now since our conception of social dignity only admits of work as being compatible with a certain few ways of living in the scale of social activities, all those that formally fell to the lot of the slaves: craftsmanship and the less important positions in commerce and industry, were automatically excluded, thus rendering our man unsuited, by lack of the sedimentation of experience, for embarking without hindrance, reserves or preconceptions, on the industrialization of the XIXth century which built up the grandeur of so many nations, less shackled than ours to the Roman and subsequently the Portuguese tradition of rule by slavery. With its abolition, we only freed ourselves from the past by thought, will and reason, continuing the while paradoxically anchored to inherent prejudices and lyrically bound to a legacy of preconceptions.

The consequences were inevitable. In a country which was at that time essentially agricultural, we cast off slave labor, the basis of our economic prosperity, without in exchange taking advantage of freely consented labor, which should have enabled us to balance the situation anew. It was as if work, whatever its nature might be so long as its ends were constructive, were forever bound up with the humiliations of slavery. To this origin may be traced the dissatisfaction of individuals with the tasks, services and positions entrusted to them, the cankering abscesses of personal susceptibility, vanities carried to extremes of morbidity, pedantism, conceit, and all the well-known repercussions thereof on our national charater. No one is satisfied with what he has got, few put their heart into what they are doing, all feel that they have been robbed of what in reality they lost on account of the ineluctable social transformations to which they did not know how to adapt themselves.

It is easy to note the result of these patrician restrictions imposed against work, on a cultural plane, particularly when they are extended to the domain of technics and specialization: instead of engineers and mechanics, we have a host of scholars, humanists, bachelors of law, arts and letters. There is no bandying with the lower forms of work necessary to commerce and industry. Such activities — any office other than that of employer — do not become a well-bred gentleman with many centuries of blue blood in his veins. Seignors of ancient lineage and their descendants have the right to perpetuate the conception of a patriarchal way of living, in the noble guise of authentic patricians not yet stripped of their ancient privileges; at the same time, however, freed slaves and their progeny are only too anxious to obliterate the marks of their origin, and therefore nurture the same objection as their former seignors to work, craftsmanship, trade, industry, mechanization, and literature with constructive ends in view.

Result: with the crumbling of its *point d'appui*, all the social and economic framework of Brazilian society as it was, a patriarchal structure based on land-ownership and slavery, was fated to collapse, thereby retarding our definitive incorporation in the style of life which was even then maturing, to our great scandal and surprise.

VI

The Bahian cult of erudition or, more exactly, the Brazilian cult of erudition, might be taken as a congenital malady of the various cultural nuclei of Brazilian literature, did we not know that it is conditioned and eased off by our social formation itself. Thus in Amazonia it has been corrected and fashioned by the elemental influence of Nature, and in the Northeast by sociological tendencies; in Minas it has been driven out by geographical considerations.

Minas, from this aspect, would, I am sure, be the delight of a writer like Taine. Not that I believe implicitly in Taine. I do not believe in Taine, any more than I believe in Gobineau, nor Chamberlain, nor any of those servitors of the racial temple who are to be held remotely responsible for the collective neurosis of pan-Germanism, any more than I believe in systematicians in general. To all of them, I prefer Paracelsus, the alchemist, with his theory of the *genius loci,* embryonic, perhaps, of the imposing generalizations of Spengler. This, however, in no way prevents me from recognizing, in the case of Taine, the value of the geographic factors, within certain limits. In Minas, they are irrefutable. In other sections of the country, geographical stardards may be set aside. In relation to Minas, they can not. The geography of the region thrusts itself into the foreground. Set in a network of mountains, the country districts, or *municípios*, separated from each other by walls of granite like a succession of huge amphitheaters, each live a life apart. For this reason, *municipalism,* which embodies the idea of an individual township squatting in the center of a deckle-edge patch of rich surrounding country, lies at the heart of the history of Minas, molding its inhabitants to an eminently *municipal* type in the Brazilian sense of the term. It is difficult to speak of a man from Minas, however great may be the national repercussion of his value, without thinking of the *município* to which he belongs. Generally an introvert, a man of little spontaneity, wrapped in the silence of his own thoughts, and to whom may as a rule be attributed all those defects etched by Taine into his analysis of the mountaineer, the *Mineiro,* our man from Minas, was bound to betray the influence of municipalism in his literary work. By municipalism, we mean his lack of interest in the repercussion of his literary effort and his inaptitude for proselytism. For even literature, a cultural pursuit the merit of which the *Mineiro* generally exaggerates, is practised by him with a certain air of inward rebellion. In fact, the literature of Minas, from Cláudio Manuel da Costa to Tomás

Antônio Gonzaga, invariably oscillates between these two poles: tacit revolt and overestimation of the value of culture, with the result that, for the former motive, Anibal Machado has refused for many years to publish a book which his friends deem to be excellent, and the latter incited Afonso Arinos to spend years in compiling *O Índio Brasileiro e a Revolução Francesa* (The Brazilian Indian and the French Revolution), a perfect gem of the XVIIIth century, cast adrift in contemporary literature. Again, both tendencies are to be found in the poems of Carlos Drummond de Andrade, as much as in the prose of Ciro dos Anjos. Tacit revolt, municipalism — I repeat: municipalism in the sense of inaptitude for proselytism and lack of interest in the destiny and aims of a work of art — and overestimation of the value of culture, sum up the cultural nucleus of Minas.

VII

A great difference, from the point of view of proselytism, is to be found in the literature of São Paulo. Whereas the *Mineiro* hedges himself about with his municipalism, the inhabitant of São Paulo, the *Paulista*, faithful to the tradition of his pioneer ancestors, the *bandeirantes,* seldom or never loses sight of the imperial significance of the *bandeiras*. This mustering of *bandeirantes* for a pioneer expedition has ever been the vocation of the *Paulista,* who is an adventurer at heart.

From the very plateau, whence the winding caravans set forth to stretch ever farther the boundaries of the growing country, in the conquest of Brazil for Brazil's sake, it is only mete that the *bandeiras* should once again ride out on this or that great, nationwide intellectual campaign. The *bandeira*, the tendency to proselytise on every plane: geographical, economical, political, social and cultural — herein lies the *genus loci* of São Paulo. Everything there is imbued with this imperial idea of conquest. As soon as the *Paulista* gets a grip on an idea, he immediately wants to see it propagated all over the country. Thus we have Monteiro Lobato, undoubtedly the most representative of all the writers of São Paulo. Scarcely has he discovered the tangled complex of conditions that is slowing down the progress of the country, than all doubts are cast to the winds: they are undermining her health, beating down her will-power, diminishing her stock of resistence, softening her character.... All this and more is spread-eagled to the country symbolically but transparently. The national symbol, Jeca Tatú, is born — the only true symbol of the masses that Brazilian literature has ever created. The creation of a symbol is one of the few really important things in a literature, if not the most important of all. For without symbols the great pile of books that crowd the shelves of national libraries from century to century, would lose much of its significance. Where would Greek literature be without Ulysses? That of Spain without Don Quixote? That of England without Hamlet? Germany without Faust? France without Tartufe? I will not go so far as to maintain that Jeca Tatú is, like them, a symbol destined to go down to perpetuity, but so long as the conditions that brought him into being, last, he will not perish and for an accurate comprehension of our problems, he will be worth more than all the reports which our great administrative intelligences prepare every year for the ultimate satisfaction of the grubs that batten on their archives. And I do not think that I exaggerate my impressions, when I affirm that with the symbol of Jeca Tatú the social problem of Brazil has been set before the country for it to reflect thereon, whereas for a very long time it had been relegated to the level of routine police work.

I have cited the case of Monteiro Lobato. I might cite others, since in every Paulista of mark there is always a *bandeirante*, full-fledged or in perspective. Naturally, this noble tendency has its counterfeitors like any other. Degenerate forms of bandeirism are bound to arise from time to time; under the pretex of carrying civilization and culture to the distant confines of Brazil, they merely aim at the conquest of the country, so as to drag her down to the common denominator of barbarianism. In Alexandria also, previous to the bar-

barian invasion — so historians of distinction inform us — there arose every now and then one of these new formulas with which market day miracle men in epileptoid harangues of pure verbalism attempt to astound the public. Perhaps they also christtened their mascarades with the name of movement. But such degenerate forms of bandeirism do not prevent the recurrent inception in São Páulo of movements of the highest social and cultural importance.

The modernist movement, for instance, the first step towards the transformations through which Brazil has passed in the last fifteen years. . . . One fine day, among the élite of São Paulo, a few young people realized with enthusiasm that it was necessary to shake the country free from its apathy, to make war on taboos, to destroy the old bonzes in their shrines, to set up new standards, to cast down a few idols from their pedestals. With no clear idea of what they wanted, they knew very well what they did not want. They no longer wanted the sonnet. They no longer wanted the sun to be "the orb of day", nor the moon to be "Cynthia, sweet regent of the night" or in classic Portuguese: "the Ophelic watch-tower of the distracted wayfarer". In the midst of all this, shoulder to shoulder with intelligences of real value, such as Cassino Ricardo and Mário de Andrade, many a Corybant sang wild melodies, many a self-styled discoverer vociferated of new cults, new gods, new altars and new religions, discrediting the movement. But together with an abundant and unintelligible flow of technicalities, colored with vague remembrances of the myths of savagery, something there was that had to remain. What changes were to spring from the modernist movement! Transformations that in other epochs were spread over centuries, ran their spell in less than twenty years. Up till then, authors had written in a style contemporaneous with Vieira and Manuel Bernardes. Readers delighted in Tobias Barreto whole-heartedly and Rui was learnt by heart without changing so much as a comma. Things of the outside world offered no interest apart from the measure in which they might suggest striking images with which to decorate the purple patches of a speach. The orator's chair was at a premium. Anything was accepted with avidity: open air meetings, inaugurations, banquets, funerals, marriages and christenings. How many brains were blown out for a mere peroration! We thought all this splendid, sacrosanct. After the movement, above all after some of its adepts had ventured to outline in a paragraph or so the biographies of gentlemen who were posing for four hundred pages, everything changed. We became enemies of the stereotyped phrase, we dared to apply a few restrictions to the great Rui himself. And we who were thinking with words, a pastime that should only be allowed the sonorous Italian language, began to think with ideas in our own rough and rude Portuguese tongue.

VIII

In opposition to what happens in Amazonia, where man lives constantly exposed to the onslaughts of cosmic terror, in Rio Grande do Sul, at any rate in that part of Rio Grande do Sul which has been revealed to the outside world, the land is endowed with that calm beauty that rests the senses. There man can commune with nature, raise up to her a cult of pantheistic devotion, for earth-born peril is not forever dogging his footsteps. On the contrary, everything bows and softens before his dominating will. On the plains and up on the plateau, all the southern countryside is gently carpeted in green and undulates with rolling hills. On top of the highest rises, amid groves of cinnamon trees, stand the plantation houses, white, green and blue, in rough-hewn imitations of medieval castles ready for the eventuality of struggle of any kind. All around, silence hangs in the air, with peace, sweetness and plenty. Cattle in gay patches grazing along the wire fences, islets of brushwood seeming to float in the curves of the hills. At the slightest sound, the gallop of a horse, the creak of a cart-wheel, the impudent roar of a motor, the distant barking of dogs — partridge rise from out of the high grass in low, clamorous flight, ostriches race hither and thither in startled abandon, the cattle raise slow muzzles over the barbed wire and the cry of the quero-quero bird in everlasting recrimination grows more strident.

In this Virgilian scene of shepherds and flocks, man casts his eye around and meets with no insurmountable barriers to block out the landscape; he shouts aloud and his voice is not thrown back at him, mocking and provocative, in the echo of the mountains. Here he has to be a dominator. Held by the enchantment of the land, he can but respect and obey the social organization, at the same time democratic and authoritative, of plantation and ranch, loving the work which is his by right and carrying it out with the grace and agility of an athlete practising his favorite sport. For this dominator is really in love with his surroundings. Hence his individualism, his narcissism and at times his urge to blossom out into a *caudilho,* the recognized head of a faction, which at bottom is only the exacerbation of his individualism. Hence, indeed, the regional literature, wherein there is only room for subjects of absorbing interest on the ranch: rodeos, breaking in the foals, horses, Indian girls, quero-queros, daring, stoicism, death in combat, ruined settlements, free fights, shakedown shelters, jamborees, accordeons, racing on the straight. For him, only such things are of importance, only they are worthy of respect and veneration. In literature, the barbarie tales of Simões Lopes Neto and Darci Azambuja, and the poetry of Vargas Neto, go straight like naught else to the ear and to the heart of the man of the prairies, filling all his aspirations. Free from the superiority of any man, he is for this reason vague and indifferent to the subtleties and distinctions ruling in worlds that do not belong to him. In the extreme simplicity of his vocabulary, virile in its resonance, foreigners, whether they be Uruguayan, Argentine, German, French, English or Italian, are confounded in just one term: *gringos*. In his division of Brazil and the Brazilians, the same simplicity persists: within Rio Grande do Sul, those who can ride a horse, the super-privileged, the *gaúchos;* over and beyond the State boundaries, from Santa Catarina to Amazonas, the *baianos,* though Bahia is half a continent away. It is useless to attempt to prove to them the illogical nature of their classification. They will not change things. From this state of mind it may readily be concluded that, at a time when inferiority complexes are so popular, there is no exaggeration in stating that the gaucho's complex is definitely a complex of superiority. Untroubled by envy, completely lacking in timidity, vigilant but not distrustful, the gaúcho is so indifferent to whatever may be happening outside the limits of his hills, that despite the passage of nearly a century and a quarter since the first wave of German colonization in Rio Grande do Sul, he was scarcely aware of the transformations induced thereby in the social physiognomy of the province. Scarcely had he time, indeed, to perceive that in those hundred and twenty years, the changes could not have been greater; in the course of that period, Rio Grande became industrialized and industry acquired an importance almost equal to that of livestock; the way of living was profoundly modified, as were the regional habits and customs; the patriarchal family, close knit and Brazilian, gave way to the European type of family, isolated and self-contained. It was necessary for the descendants themselves of the former colonists to denounce to Rio Grande and the nation, the threat to the ancient stock of our racial formation — the twin development of Brazilian and Portuguese culture — a denunciation which Gilberto Freire supported with the prestige and the seal of his unrivalled authority on sociological problems in his book *Uma cultura ameaçada* (A threatened culture), for the gaucho to apprehend the new realities that encircled him. Then only did he begin to perceive that in the region of valleys and rivers beyond his hills, a, new type of civilization had arisen, and with this new type of civilization located at the confluence of the Azorian, Italian and German currents of immigration, there had come a new type of culture, directed by contrast more towards the universal than towards the regional. Only then, faced with the evidence of the transition, did he resolve to admit the oscillations between regional and universal that characterize the activity of the cultural nucleus of Rio Grande do Sul at the present time.

This alternative, which may have given Lindolfo Color to the world of action and thought, may likewise have produced in the strictly literary field, writers each with his own strong blend of individualism, like Érico Veríssimo — the first to display a liking for Anglo-American influence to the detriment of Latin exclusivity —, Augusto Meyer, De Sousa Júnior, Alcides Maia — ever undecided as to whether he preferred the regional or the universal trend — or again writers like João Pinto da Silva and Paulo

Arinos, universal in their conceptions but strictly regional in their choice of motives.

I should like to include among the writers of the cultural group to which I belong, the name of Álvaro Moreira. If I do not do so, it is from a love of accuracy. In reality, Álvaro Moreira does not belong, from a cultural point of view, to Rio Grande do Sul. Thirty years ago, in the company of Felipe de Oliveira, he left his land, his relations and the house of his father, as in the Gospels, to venture out into the wide world. Both poet and a son of Rio Grande, a good deal of an orator, with his own dash of the *caudilho*, he naturally set out with two great desires locked in his breast: one human and crystal clear with the age of centuries — to dislodge Prometheus, a fellow idealist, from his Caucasian rock; the other more recent, modest and regional — to riograndecize Brazil. He failed to dislodge Prometheus, nor did he riograndecize Brazil. Gravitating to Rio de Janeiro, he donned the toga of a sceptic and a *Carioca* and became one of the most eminent exponents of the cultural nucleus of the metropolis.

IX

Finally, we come to the cultural group of the metropolis. Emanating from the capital of Brazil, this group might well be expected to be the strongest, the most elevated and the most vigorous expression of thought, bearing the greatest influence on Brazilian literature. Apart from its function as microcosm of the cultural archipelago of Brazil, wherein the representatives of each provincial nucleus are more or less numerous, its real importance is much less than is supposed. This is the explanation: not being the capital of a unitarian and strongly centralized State, like the great centers of European culture, that effectively radiate great cultural movements throughout their respective countries, Rio de Janeiro has, up till quite recently, been weighed down by a sense of tremendous ill luck: that of living in permanent subordination to one of the cultural nuclei of the provinces, at the mercy now of São Paulo, now of Minas, now of Rio Grande do Sul. Thus it may be seen that her position, although apparently predominant, while not being strictly secondary, remains on a level with that of the provincial literary centers. Rio lacks the imperial style, the arrogance of a Carthage, the conviction of her supremacy. Nor do I believe that the origin of the amiable provincial aspect that characterizes the metropolis, is to be sought for elsewhere. In the presence of this reality, the *Carioca*, charming yet inffectual inhabitant, debarred from political originality and stifled in his imperial possibilities, could but produce, not a literature of militant ideals, nor great creative ressources, but the delicate works of a painter of customs, a sceptic, an ironist. Without the constant urge of political vigor of a more ambitious cultural nucleus, the city became tolerant as a graceful woman, languoring in that lazy provincial charm that is a real joy to authentic provincials, and the *Carioca* soon learnt to quench the ardor of his messages, taking refuge in a literature descriptive of times and customs. Instead of making history, he put up with it. And in order to put up with it with resignation, he called in irony, the famous irony of the *Carioca,* which, like that described by Anatole France, smiles neither of love nor beauty; "kind and benevolent" as she is, "her laugh calms anger" and it is she that teaches us to "disdain the stupid and the spiteful", for without her aid, one might succumb to the "weakness of hating".

Herein lies the origin, under certain aspects, of the drama and irony of Machado de Assis, a drama lived more or less intensely by the metropolitan writers of our days. Can it be an absolute incapacity for public life that prevented a man of the high literary and social standing of Machado de Assis from exerting any political influence on his times? I doubt it. Whoever could take the elections at the Academy of Letters as seriously as he did, and manoeuver the members with such diabolical skill, must have had his own political bent. Politics, which he dubbed "that sterile Messalina who frees no man from the hysterical convulsions of her embrace other than broken and useless" did not always fill him with such instinctive repugnance as is generally supposed. The proof of this is that, when he found himself faced with the necessity of writing the political editorial of the *Diário do Rio,* on account of the departure of Quintino Bocaiúva for the United States, he did not feel at all out of place in this kind of literature. He even showed that he was not lacking in considerable aptitude for the verbal tourneys in which his friends triumphed. The abstention of Machado de Assis, therefore, was far more remote and far deeper in origin and must be looked for in the same political, social and cultural sources that made Lima Barreto and Marques Rebêlo, and the Carioca writers in general, prefer columns, short-story writing, and criticism of a non-militant character, to any other literary work.

The power of the cultural nucleus of Rio lies far more in her faculty for tempering and correcting the extravagance of the provinces, than strictly in her own creative urge. In this field, she is unequalled. For the relations of the capital with the provinces are paradoxical: whereas Rio has no confidence in herself, the provinces tremble before her judgments. What will Rio say? This is the attitude of the cultural nuclei of the provinces. Without passing through the filter of her criticism and receiving her approval, no expression of provincial thought can hope to conquer Brazil. Only by braving the arrows of her irony and gaining her sympathy and comprehension, can right of citizenship be attained.

This is what happened with the modernist movement. Without the approval of Rio, there is no doubt that it would have died in São Paulo. In reality, the movement had not in itself the impulse to survive. Possessed of too much critical ability, it crumbled through a lack of organic cohesion. But this predominance of critical ability over organic constructivity, before developing into the drama of the modernist movement, was already the tragedy, the immense tragedy of our times. All of us know we what do not want, no one knows what he does want. With regard to the past, the organic intelligence endeavors to conciliate it with the present, the critical intelligence hastens to shoulder it with all the calamities of today, casting down its values in an agony of destruction, bristling with an aversion for all that comes from that yesterday which weighs them down with the humiliation of dishonor and the horror of a nightmare. Hence the misfortunes and the calamities of our century, the hatred with which the past is regarded by peoples without a history, and the ruined landscape of nowadays: everywhere façades torn down and broken columns, mutilated statues, bas-reliefs and capitals shattered to pieces, and man, desperate in the frenzy of impotence as he surveys this pile of ruins, not knowing how or where to set about the work of reconstruction.

X

These seven nuclei: Amazonia, the Northeast, Bahia, Minas, São Paulo, Rio Grande do Sul and the Metropolis, are the seven keys to Brazilian literature. Not only to our literature but also to our sociogenesis. Do others exist? Perhaps, but none that can be included in the seven chief divisions. Maranhão, for instance, whose vigor might have thrust it up to a group apart, has always oscillated, after the fashion of Sergipe with João Ribeiro and Gilberto Amado, between two poles: Bahia and the Northeast, when indeed it has not been characterized by a harmonization of the two. Bahia it was that attracted Coelho Neto, while Aloísio Azevedo leant towards the Northeast; Graça Aranha swayed back and forth from the Northeast to Bahia; Sergipe mingles with Bahia and the Northeast in the works of João Ribeiro, a regular miracle of fusion in the cultural climate of the Metropolis where the two tendencies meet. The State of Rio, as opposed to the Federal District, is pure Northeast in creative forms, style of life and social trends — a condition which is probably linked up with the fact that Euclides da Cunha, Alberto Tôrres and Oliveira Viana come therefrom.

I admit that it is impossible even superficially to exhaust the possibilities of this subject within the narrow limits of a lecture. In the case of Bahia, I have examined but one aspect of the question without stressing its antithesis, that is, the contrary of the regional eruditeness, as shown in the works of Nina Rodriguez, Hermes Lima and others, for, when all is said and done, there is an opposite to everything. But generally speaking, I am convinced that I have been neither extravagant nor unjust, despite the affirmation that a man of one culture is not fitted to comprehend with sympathetic discernment the manifestations of another cultural school, to which he does not belong.

There can be no doubt about it: the great realities of Brazil reside in these seven cultural islands. Far be it from me to proclaim that they are our only realities and the exclusive causes of our social phenomena. Far be it from me to fall back into the error of those who examine cultural and social phenomena in the light of laws and reasoning of the mechanical world, wherein everything comes under the sway of the undeviating fatality of the principle of cause and effect.

Systematizers in general and historical materialists in particular, tend to proclaim from the very beginning that history develops exclusively around the economic factor, only to reduce this exclusivity to a position of modest predominance as they go on, whereas in reality it is impossible to speak of predominance or exclusivity, in that one cannot reduce the forces of social reality to a common denominator, with a view to comparison. Their failure is a warning. Shortening sail as I speed towards generalization, I merely announce that the seven islands of our cultural archipelago are the great realities of Brazil; that this conception enables our social trends and events, whether historical, economic, political or literary, to stand out clear against the obscure background of other ways of thinking and all their intricate confusion. These seven cultural nuclei are equally efficacious in explaining our struggles of separatist tendency and our rivalities, both small and great, in the world of letters; the revolution of Rio Grande in 1835 and that of São Paulo in 1932; the Indianism, rising in the North from a social urge, and the modernist movement emanating from São Paulo in the adventurous form of a *bandeira;* the close solidarity linking together the writers of the Northeast and the isolated worlds in which the writers of the extreme South develop their individualism; great facts and minor incidents. When Silvio Romero attempts to tarnish the glory of Machado de Assis, in favor of Tobias Barreto, that he would like to see converted into a sort of basis for a literary metric system to be applied to Brazil, he is merely enhancing the merits of the cultural nucleus to which he belongs; similarly, Labieno, pseudonym which conceals the name of the *Mineiro,* Lafaiete Rodrigues Pereira, entering the lists with his admirable *Vindiciæ,* is acting in honor and defense of the cultural nucleus to which his own is so intimately linked. And more recently, the disapproval of Álvaro Lins for *Dirceu e Marília* (Dirceu and Marília), by Afonso Arinos de Melo Franco, merely betrays his Pernambuco and Northeastern origin for he also is acting in accordance with the tenets of his group, which cannot admit the emphasis of the sentimental and lyrical element of drama, at the expense of the political and social significance, where for his part Afonso Arinos is only following the guiding lines of the group of Minas, when he underestimates the social aspect and attaches particular value to the strictly literary treatment of the subject.

To sum up: all of us, some more, others less, consciously or unconsciously, are acting within the orbit of our cultural nuclei. It is useless, therefore, to theorize as to whether this constitutes an evil or a quality, because, whether good or bad, it remains an irrefutable reality. But the true theory admits of no doubt: what appears to be an evil, because apparently it limits us, is the true source of our highest and purest values. Separated from his cultural nucleus, unless it remains deep-rooted in his soul, the writer, whatever may be the roads opening up before him in life, runs the risk of being perverted. He may keep the mastery of his technique, and yet the inner flame of his inspiration may die low. The man without a cultural nucleus, like the being without a home or a country, is a eutopia when he is not an object of degradation. Alas, for those who allow themselves to be morally uprooted, for those who do not carry, imponderable in the thread of their garments, the dust of their provincial nucleus, that dust of culture that we glean not only from the books we read, but also from the air we breathe, the images we contemplate, the human types, with which our early years are passed, the crosses that watch over the eternal rest of our sacred dead, our village church bells, the virtues and the defects of our starting-place in life. It is true that general and universal ideas are excellent, but once the hour of philosophies and utopias is passed

— and they pass terribly soon — without the common denominators of our cultural nuclei, without the echo of the spheres that brought us up, we remain stumbling in the void, void ourselves and aimless. Ulysses abandoning the paradise of Ogygia, and the personage of Tierra del Fuego returning to the land of his birth, are alike symbols of the fidelity which marks the measure of great creations. In order to achieve greatness and universality, Shakespeare did not have to deny his England, nor Cervantes his Alcalá de Henares, nor Dante his Florence. All belonged to their lands and their times.

XI

Would that Brazilian writers were of their times, as they are of their land and their cultural nuclei. But, Alas! we live permanently beset by the alternative: either to live behind the times or to flee with them. Still saturated with patriarchal preconceptions, if our taste be considered, we would willingly barter the specialization of nowadays for the universalism of the XVIIIth century. Not that we have not yet understood, in all the extent of its urgency, the necessity for changing course. Faced with the menace that lours over the social edifice of the West, and particularly of Brazil, we are all more or less persuaded that if we do not wish to perish under the ruins, we cannot and must not remain in aweful idleness, contemplating the desolation of the panorama, scattered with débris and overshadowed with such somber perspectives. We cannot content ourselves with being purely critical; we must become organically constructive.

Let us remain true to our cultural nuclei, catch up with the faith and way of living of our times, intoxicate ourselves with the essential truth that a civilization is an ever-progressive conquest, in the spirit of an epoch, and we shall possess the Brazil that looms through the mists of the future, with a literature worthy of this great achievement; a literature that must be earth-wracked, like Amazonia; social, like the Northeast; erudite, like Bahia; humanist, like Minas; pioneer, like São Paulo; both regional and universal, like Rio Grande do Sul; all this tempered by the irony of the cultural nucleus of the capital, so that it may be, above all, in accordance with our finest desires, profoundly human and Brazilian.